100+ Free Content for Social Media & Web

Don't Spend Money on Tools and Resources You Can Use for Free

Anita Nipane

I recommend not checking out all tools and resources at once as it's a lot of information and you will enjoy this book a lot more if you don't get overloaded.

This book was written by Anita Nipane of Digginet.

Copyright © 2021 by Anita Nipane.

All rights reserved. No part of this book may be used or reproduced in any manner whatsoever without written permission except in the case of brief quotations embodied in critical articles or reviews.

Trademarks

All product and brand names identified throughout this book are used for their benefit with no intention of infringement of their copyrights. No such use is intended to convey endorsement or other affiliation with this book.

For information, contact: http://www.digginet.com

Contents

Free Online Tools Series

Book Nr. 2

GET IT ON AMAZON

Is this book for you?

Do you need to create engaging   visual   content for social media, webpage, or blog?

The good news is – you don't need to hire a designer or buy expensive software to create visuals for the web. You can do it YOURSELF and with FREE tools, thanks to the wide variety of resources available on the Internet. There are so many easy and quick solutions out there! Actually, even the most highly paid pros take help from the same resources you are going to learn in this book.

After reading this book, you will be able to:

- get royalty-free images and video footage even for commercial purposes
- customize photos, create visuals and animated banners for social media and web
- take and edit screenshots as well as record tutorial videos from your screen
- remove background from any image (no Photoshop or design skills needed)
- create engaging memes and infographics
- add beautiful and free fonts to your computer to use them in your designs

- edit videos, add animations, and create intros and outros for your YouTube videos
- "steal" color codes from any website and pick tasteful color combinations for your brand and web banners
- create a unique logo for your brand and generate your company's brand book in minutes
- use other tools that will save your time and improve efficiency

In brief, you'll be able to create visuals for your webpage, blog, and social media yourself and with no money spent. This book will be a toolset that you can use as a manual every time you need to find a free online tool to create marketing content. Actually, I'm using it like my manual, too and I'm happy to share it with you.

P.S. You will notice some of the tools are mentioned several times in different sections of this book. That's because they have diversified functionality and can be used for different purposes.

Enjoy!

46 Amazing Sites with Free Stock Photos

Almost every design starts with a picture. And as we all know; a single picture can be worth a thousand words. But where do you find free images for your website design, blog, social media post, or a simple ad design without spending a lot of money for it? Of course, if you can afford it, you can buy such images on websites like istock.com, shutterstock.com, or any other similar sites. If you know how to, you can create images by yourself, too. However, quality pictures can also be found online for free – without investing much work into creating them, and at the same time not infringing any copyrights.

There are many portals on the Internet that offer free quality photos. Some of the authors ask for attribution, some of them allow using their pictures only for personal use, but there are also plenty of those who allow using their photos and images for commercial use (look for CCO license). In some cases, restrictions may apply; therefore, you should always check the license terms first, but in most cases, you can use these pictures for your blog posts, website, and social media, free of charge.

I have listed here 46 resources, where you can get free images and photos for your personal or commercial use either with attribution to the author or without it. Check them out and find your favorite one.

Searchable photo databases that offer photos for commercial use and no attribution required.

1. **pixabay.com** – more than 310 000 pictures – photos, vectors, and artistic illustrations. You can use every single one of them, both in digital and printed format, including commercial use.
2. **unsplash.com** - a library of 1 million good quality stock photographs, all available to use for free.
3. **dreamstime.com** – offers a Free Photos section with a great collection of free good-quality photos.
4. **finda.photo** – search through thousands of free stock photos across multiple free and paid stock photo sites - from one tab!
5. **freeimages.com** - more than 388 000 free photos and illustrations.
6. **morguefile.com** – stunning landscapes, animals, food, fruit, vegetables, backgrounds, and also artistic pictures with an abstract meaning.
7. **stockvault.net** – 62,000 free images. A great resource for your non-commercial website or blog.

8. **snapwiresnaps.tumblr.com** – free photos from 200,177 of the world's top photographers.

9. **pexels.com** – over 4,500 free stock photos. Every week at least 70 new high-resolution photos are added.

10. **picjumbo.com** – simple navigation and a huge image library. Many beautiful pictures of food and drinks, which might be very useful for marketing a restaurant or a bar.

11. **fancycrave.com** – high-resolution food, nature, people, architecture, and other photos from professional photographers.

12. **en.freejpg.com.ar** – great image source for technology, people, texture, travel, religion, and other images – more than 10 000 images.

13. **goodfreephotos.com** – a gallery of thousands of unique and free public domain stock photos. Categorized by location for travel photos, species for animal and plant photos, and types of objects for other photos.

14. **publicdomainpictures.net** – 117,700 free images. If you intend to use an image you find here for commercial use, please be aware that some photos do require a model or property release.

15. **immediateentourage.com** – offers already cut out objects on a transparent background in PNG format, as well as sketchups and textures. Worth checking out!

16. **isorepublic.com** – high-resolution images and videos. Categories: architecture, nature, people, texture, urban, and others.

17. **designerspics.com** – photos captured by the photographer Jeshu John from a port city, Kochi, in southern India.

18. **foodiesfeed.com** – a resource of free realistic food images in high resolution and free digital goods related to food.

19. **gratisography.com** – free high-resolution nature, objects, people, urban and whimsical pictures you can use on your personal and commercial projects.

20. **negativespace.co** – beautiful pictures for every use.

21. **splitshire.com** – amazing photos in 22 categories. Worth checking out.

22. **lifeofpix.com** – mostly travel and nature photos for personal and commercial use.

23. **largephotos.net** – a great source of free, high-quality large photos in different subjects and genres.

24. **magdeleine.co/browse** – photos can be sorted by those that require attribution and those that don't (CC0 –Public Domain).

25. **publicdomainarchive.com** – explore and discover treasures by great photographers. A place, where you can find inspiration and photography that you can re-use in your projects.

26. **stokpic.com** – a wide variety of photos in 16 categories.

27. **freerangestock.com** – good photos by a community of creative and talented photographers.

28. **rgbstock.com** is a free stock image site created by photographers and graphic artists with a wide variety of categories and subcategories. Registration required.

29. **pickupimage.com** – mostly nature and outdoors photos and cliparts, for example, play cards, sports, etc.

30. **freenaturestock.com** – great quality photo collection of nature and animals.

31. **stocksnap.io** – beautiful free stock photos. Hundreds of high-resolution images are added weekly.

32. **picography.co** – free hi-resolution travel and nature photos.

33. **focastock.com** – flowers, nature, and summer photos taken by photographer Jeffrey Betts.

34. **jeshoots.com** – great quality nature, animals, food, people, and devices photos.

Photo Collections without Search Option

In this list, you will find small, but beautiful and original photo collections that should be browsed manually, since no search option is provided.

35. **startupstockphotos.com** – Free photos for startups, bloggers, publishers, websites, designers, developers, creators, & everyone else.

36. **jaymantri.com** – beautiful photo collection by photographer Jay Mantri.

37. **travelcoffeebook.com** – beautiful photos of travel moments.

38. **bigfoto.com** – you will be able to download free photos of the country of your interest, including photos of hotels, and popular tourism objects.

39. **freemediagoo.com** – backgrounds, textures and photos of aviation, beach, buildings, finance, food, and wildlife.

Other

If you don't mind attributing the author and embedding a link to your chosen image or if you need a clipart or some vintage image, then check out this list.

40. **flickr.com** – a huge variety of photos by amateurs and professional photographers. Always check the license terms of each photo – in most cases attribution is required. You can share the image you like on social media and your website with the image link.

41. **compfight.com** – a Flickr image search engine that helps you find images based on your license needs. Most of the images require attribution.

42. **search.creativecommons.org** – a sort of photo search engine that helps find images, videos, and music on 12 web portals, like, Flickr, Google, Youtube, and others. To be sure that you

can use the media for your chosen purpose, always verify the license terms of each image.

43. **commons.wikimedia.org/wiki/Category:Images** – is a database of 21,049,775 freely usable media files to which anyone can contribute.

44. **ancestryimages.com** – offers a free image archive of historical prints, maps, and artifact photos.

45. **nos.twnsnd.co** – a collection of vintage photos from the public archives you can use for personal and non-commercial purposes. Most require attribution.

46. **openclipart.org** – high variety of clip arts for unlimited commercial use.

Picture Copyrights Explained

There are three main groups of licenses you should know about.

1. **Creative Commons (or CC) license** - is the most widespread Open Content licensing model. There are six Creative Commons license types. I won't list them all but if you know them, you can read about the terms of each license on the official Creative Commons webpage: https://creativecommons.org/licenses. The main thing you always need to check out before deciding to use an image, font, or video for your marketing content, is whether it can be used for commercial use and requires attribution or not. If the item is listed under CC0 license, it means that you can freely edit, distribute and publish it both for personal or commercial use. There are no rights reserved. Another popular license is CC1. In this case, you can use the resource only if you give appropriate credit to the owner according to requirements. They usually are described on the site where you find them. However, bear in mind that some rules still apply: you cannot use Creative Common pictures or videos with identifiable people (face clearly seen) in a way that they may find offensive, unless they give their consent. If you use pictures with people, logos, private property, etc.,

make sure they are suitable for your application and don't infringe anybody's rights.

2. **Royalty-Free license** –allows you to use a picture, video, or font without the need to pay royalties or license fees for each use. Basically, it means that you pay for it only once and then you can use it as many times as you like. However, some restrictions apply. For example, you are not allowed to "borrow" a picture from a friend who has bought it, because this license cannot be transmitted. Only the account owner who bought the picture, is allowed to use it. Royalty-Free licensed images can be used on websites, for educational projects, in booklets, magazines, newspapers, flyers, games. In general, you can use them in any advertising and promotional material, in either printed or electronic media.

3. **Extended License** – if you are going to use a picture for creating either a digital or tangible product that you are going to sell in big amounts, you will need to buy this license - which is much more expensive than the previous one. Examples of such products are: web templates, greeting cards or postcards, print-on-demand services, like, canvas, t-shirts, mugs, mouse pads, and other similar products.

Bear in mind, that different websites can have slightly different licensing terms. Always read them, before you buy the picture, font, or video. If you are not sure, whether you can use it for your purpose, contact the website's support and clarify it.

7 Tools to Change Background of Photo Online

If you have experienced the situation where you need to remove the background of a picture, you know how frustrating it can be. If you don't have a professional image editing software like Photoshop, it can even feel like mission impossible. And, even if you have one, you may need to spend a lot of time, learning how to correctly remove the background from the image. However, it is not as complicated as it may seem at first glance. The truth is that there are many online photo background removers available. Here are a few of them.

1. **online.photoscissors.com** – it's an interactive cutout tool for removing background from pictures. Simply upload your image, mark the foreground and background areas and their algorithm takes care of the details. Use the feathering function to smooth the edges. You can also change the background color – either to a solid color of your choice or upload a new background image. Save your picture as a PNG file. It's free. The disadvantage is that it cannot be used for big files. The maximum file size is 5 MB.

2. **removal.ai** – a free background remover that removes image background 100% automatically using AI technology. Just drag and drop your photo, count 1, 2, 3 and download the

1500 x 1000 px resolution image with transparent background for FREE. Although the photo editor is simple, it has most of the tools that you will need to be creative. Aside from the usual cropping, resizing, and manual eraser, you can also add a new background to your photo. Rather impressive!

3. **burner.bonanza.com** - quickly removes the background from any image or photo. First remove the background automatically, then you can touch up your image manually to improve the result. Simply sign in and edit your images. Also has its paid version for professionals – starting from 9.95 $/month.

4. **www10.lunapic.com** - go to Edit->Transparent and select the color you want to remove. May be a good solution for removing a solid color background, but not so convenient for multicolor backgrounds.

5. **Ultimate Background Eraser** for Android (get on Google Play Store) – there are several background eraser apps on Google Play Store and all of them have rather similar functionality and features. I tested several of them, but this one was the most effective. You can use either its magic wand feature that removes the area of similar color automatically or select a particular area to remove specific areas. A cool feature is that this app shows a magnifying glass every time you press the screen. It is like zoom but only works in a particular area where you are pressing your finger.

Therefore, it's much easier to make adjustments. Moreover, when finished, you can add text and emojis to personalize it.

6. **Magic Eraser Background Editor for Apple** users (get on Apple App Store) - removes the background of any picture with just a few taps and saves as PNG or JPG. Just touch where you want to remove, and the "Magic Wand" function removes the area of similar color automatically.

7. However, my favorite tool that I use for removing image backgrounds is **PowerPoint**. As you can see from the video below, it is very easy to use. If you already have PowerPoint on your computer, you don't need any other tools. Of course, it won't provide a perfect PhotoShop quality, but it will give a result good enough for web banners and social posts. Watch the tutorial on YouTube. The same functionality is also available in Microsoft Word.

6 Image Editing Online Tools You Should Know About

Social media and blog posts with pictures usually bring much better results than simple texts without any visual material or poorly designed and bad looking images. Therefore, it is important to create good quality images that attract your target audience. The good news is that these days you don't need a lot of money or professional design service to create a visual for your website or social media. Actually, it is a feasible task for every Internet or smartphone user, and it can be done almost or completely for free using online image editors. You don't even need to install any specific software. **Tasks that used to take designers hours now can be done in just a few clicks.**

All you need is to use one of these image editing tools.

1. One of such tools is **canva.com.** It makes creating designs amazingly simple and fun even if you're not a designer. Use its pre-made templates, backgrounds, effects, and a gallery of various pictures to create quote images, simple infographics, book covers, greeting cards, and many other designs. Start creating your designs at no cost, use a paid monthly plan, or buy their lifetime Pro plan. Worth a try!

2. **pixlr.com** is an excellent substitute for complex photo

editing tools like Photoshop even if you have no much technical photo editing experience. It allows you to work with layers, replace color, clone background, transform objects, and much more. Moreover, you can download it as an app for your smartphone and use it straight away.

3. **easil.com** - an easy-to-use drag-and-drop design tool that helps you create content for social media, web, and print: posters, flyers, menus, infographics, and more. Works both on desktops and smartphones.

4. **pixelied.com** - ready-made thumbnails, header images, story and post graphics, and more for all your marketing channels. With this tool, you can retouch e-commerce product images, replace backgrounds, and easily create branded designs for social media, blog posts, and other content.

5. **befunky.com** is an image editing tool that will help you make fully customized graphic designs, add interesting effects, create great collages and flawless selfies. You can use their templates or do everything from scratch.

6. Install **Adobe Photoshop Express App** (iOS/Android/Windows Phone), and you will get some Photoshop functionality on your smartphone for free. You will be able to crop, straighten, rotate, flip, color, remove red eye and use such filters like Vibrant, Superpunch, and Glow. Plus, you can add borders and frames to the photos. A quick solution for editing

pictures on your smartphone.

As you can see, there are many online tools that you can use for image creation and photo editing. And you don't have to be a professional designer to do that. However, it is very important to know the main principles of composition, color theory, and typeface usage to create really good-looking designs. Therefore, I highly suggest you read my book - **Graphic Design for Beginners: Fundamental Graphic Design Principles that Underlie Every Design Project**, because that will help you to avoid amateurish mistakes and your designs will become more effective and attractive.

8 Best Photo Editor Apps - Create Beautiful Images on Your Smartphones

If you use social media to promote your business, you need to have great eye-catching photos to attract your audience and get those desired likes and engagements. Most photos need improvements to look really attractive. In order to improve your shots, you might need to improve their contrast, saturation, brightness, or other characteristics. Alternatively, you may wish to add something catchy to the picture, for example, a sticker, some text, or a frame. Fortunately, this can be easily solved with the help of **photo editing apps** that you can use instantly on your smartphone (search in Google Play or Apple aps).

1. **adobe.com/products/photoshop-express.html**

Photoshop Express is one of the best photo editing apps on Android out there – for some reasons. Firstly, it is easy and quick to use, plus, it has a minimalistic interface. Also, it works as a powerful editing app on several devices. It offers several important features that allow you to rotate, flip, and crop your pictures. Photoshop Express also comes with one-touch filters, auto-fix, frames, colors, effects as well as several advanced tools to modify large files like panoramic images. Looking to reduce unwanted grain and speckling in your night picture? Trust the Noise Reduction feature in this photo editor app to do the trick. And here is great news – Photoshop Express can be downloaded for free, and it is ad-free.

2. adobe.com/products/fix.html

Another exciting and useful photo editor app on Android from Adobe is **Photoshop Fix**. This app can also be downloaded without charges. Some of the most popular features can be found in the desktop version of this app. As the name suggests, the ability of this app is centered on "fixing" and retouching images by playing around with the contrast, filtering, and extra effects. Photoshop Fix is equipped with useful tools that allow you to edit even facial features. For instance, you can make your smile bigger, edit your facial points, or trim down your cheeks easily. That's not all, you can play around with the saturation, exposure, and contrast to create a nice effect, plus you can get people's attention to a specific angle by blurring other parts of the image.

3. picsart.com/apps/picsart-photo-studio

With the **PicsArt Photo Studio**, you can edit, add text, make effects, and draw on your photos with ease. Also, the app allows you to have customized arrangements and setups, such as cropping images, filters, and blending. PicsArt enjoys huge popularity, with over 100 million downloads – no wonder it is considered as one of the favorite photo editing apps on Android in the current year. One of the major reasons PicsArt has accrued so many downloads is its wide range of useful options, which allow a user to customize a picture to his or her taste. Also, this photo editing app on Android comes with a built-in camera option, as well as the option to share photos directly on social media platforms. Collage, draw, stickers, and frames are some of the other fascinating features available on PicsArt. Although the app can be downloaded for free, you may need to make some in-app buys. Lastly, you will need to deal with in-app ads.

4. Toolwiz Photo-Pro Editor (get on Google Play)

This app is one of the most sophisticated photo editing apps for Android out there, considering that it packs over 200 tools. With **Toolwiz Photo-Pro Editor**, you can swap faces on your photo, adjust the saturation, filter images, and choose from exciting collages. The ToolWiz Photo-Pro Editor is free, and you will find its elegant and minimalistic interface user-friendly.

5. fotor.com/mobile.html

Compared to other image editing tools, **Fotor** has several outstanding features like the ability to enhance images easily using a one-tap tool, and options to rotate, brighten, crop, and saturate your picture. You can also add shadow, temperature, exposure, vignette, tint, and contrast. The best thing about this photo editing app on Android is probably the multitude of filters available to the user.

6. Photo Effects Pro (Get on Google Play or Apple App Store)

If you love to play with effects, stickers, filters, and similar customization options, then, **Photo Effects Pro** is your go-to-get option. This photo editing app on Android has over 40 filters and effects. In addition to frames and stickers, you can add text to your pictures. Unlike other photo editing apps on Android, this app can be used to finger paint an image and end up with something unique. While it has a small set of editing tools, the effects of these tools are enough to do the trick. Like most photo editing apps on this list, Photo Effects Pro is easy to use and free to download.

7. pixlr.com/mobile

Pixlr is among the top photo editing apps on Android with a great one-touch enhancement tool. The app is a sophisticated photo editor; it packs several features and tools. With just a click, you can use the Auto-Fix option to blend multiple colors and layers from different images to create a unique image. Also, you can become an artist with Pixlr by using its ink sketch, pencil, and poster options. Beautify your sketches with simple edit tools that allow you to get rid of blemishes while whitening your teeth.

8. Snapseed (Get on Google Play or Apple App Store)

Snapseed is another fascinating photo editing app on Android. It is sophisticated, no doubt, with several unique features that are hardly found in other apps. You have a one-touch enhancement tool and several sliders that give you the power to customize to your taste. There is a tool section where you can do most of the editing work by playing around with the common tools as well as vignette, glamor glow filters, and the magical healing brush. Snapseed also packs some great photo frames, grunge, and textures. The lighting effects offer great transformations. If you want, you can crop images, adjust white balance, rotate a picture, or fix skewed lines through the perspective filter. Snapseed is simple yet powerful, and it is free to download; has no ads or in-app purchases.

All the photo editor apps discussed above are artistic masterpieces that can tune your image to perfection. Feel free to choose any of them, depending on your preferences. Whatever your option is, rest assured of transforming your pictures to suit your taste.

6 Free Online Tools to Quickly Create Quote Images

Inspiring quote images are getting more and more popular on social media. They are a good way to engage your audience and increase your brand's popularity and reach. I have listed **6 online tools** here, and you can easily use them to create your own quote images that look beautiful and shareable on social media. Check them out and choose your favorite!

1. buffer.com/pablo

Just upload your picture, your logo, and write your text. Format it, experiment with the effects and when you are satisfied, download or publish your image directly. They automatically offer the right sizes for different social media.

2. quotescover.com

Turn any ordinary saying texts into a beautiful typography art picture for sharing on social media. Use your quote or one of theirs, choose your format, style and create a beautiful and engaging design.

3. getstencil.com

Create beautiful images using their proposed quotes and backgrounds or use your text and upload your images. In their free version, you can create and save up to 10 images a month. To use their full functionality, you will need to upgrade to their paid plan.

4. fotor.com

Provides many free and well-designed quote image templates for you to use and customize with their drag and drop editor. You don't need to be a professional designer to share your thoughts or words with pictures.

5. pixteller.com/quote-maker

With PixTeller's free online quote maker, you can create your custom quote pictures fast and easy, directly from your browser without any design skills.

6. keepcalm-o-matic.co.uk

Create your own classic Keep Calm memes or choose from already existing ones. You can also use the premade quote images – just change the font, if you feel it's necessary.

5 Meme Generators to Make Your Own Meme

Nowadays, memes take a major part of our online experience, especially on social media sites. While people think memes are only for fun and entertainment, many businesses realize that memes are effective attention grabbers and communication starters that can be used to their advantage.

Creating memes is not complicated. There are meme generators that businesses and individuals can use for their audience growth and social media success. Let's take a look at some of the top meme generators that you can use for the creation of funny, attractive, and smart memes.

1. picsart.com/meme-generator

PicsArt has all the tools required for making attractive memes and other visuals for social media. Simply choose one of their templates, add your texts, pictures and download your work.

2. imgflip.com/memegenerator

Imgflip is a website that will let you generate memes with ease. This website is a good one for those who don't want to get involved in any complicated image creation and want the work done instantly.

3. kapwing.com/meme-maker

This application is a video, image, and gif editing tool that has a lot of detailed features and functionality. Though simple memes can be generated in moments using this app, it offers a lot more for proper video and image making as well.

4. memegenerator.net

This website is exactly what its name indicates. It is an online meme generator that has thousands of meme templates that you can use to create your memes in less than a minute.

5. mematic.net

Another well-known meme generator app that will allow you to make the funniest and the most engaging memes even on your smartphone. It is very simple in terms of its interface and offers all the tools required for making a quality meme.

4 Tools to Create Educational and Interactive Infographics

Well-designed infographics are an effective way of displaying content to attract the attention of your target audience to convey statistics easily and oftentimes otherwise boring information. Actually, the process of creating a design for an infographic is not as easy as it may seem. It is one of the most complicated design projects because it is rather difficult to find a style and elements that would work for the particular infographic. This is why using premade templates could be of great help to both unprofessional and professional designers.

One of the simplest tools for creating infographics is **canva.com.** Just choose the template you like and add your content. No special design skill is needed. Infographic maker tools **easel.ly** and **piktochart.com** have similar functionality. Add your data, elements and create beautiful infographics.

If you need to create interactive charts for your webpage, **Google Charts** will be a great solution. You can choose from different chart types and templates, then add data and customize them. When finished, just copy the snippet code and paste it into your webpage administration tool as an HTML code. Then open your webpage in your Internet browser and enjoy your interactive charts.

Top 6 Book Cover Creators - Make your eBook Cover for Free

Whether you need a book cover for your lead magnet, business report, or book, a homemade, DIY book cover is a practical solution. Use one of the **book cover creators** that are listed below and cut your designer costs. These tools will provide ready-to-use templates that you can customize according to your book genre and message you want to convey to your readers.

1. canva.com

This is one of the most popular image editors in the market. It is free and subscription-based and it allows you to design various graphics and mini-presentations. It has all the options you need to make your book cover with minimal effort and design expertise. Canva is a very neat web-based and app-based tool that you can use to edit and design images you might want to use for your book covers. It is like the distilled version of Photoshop that gives you exactly what you need without all of the complexities of Photoshop.

2. placeit.com

With no design skills whatsoever, you can take advantage of Placeit book cover creator to design your cover art quickly and easily. You don't need to download any additional software as everything is done on the website. With this platform, you are taking full control of your design process and it really couldn't get any easier than Placeit makes it. They have a ton of design templates that you can play with until you settle for something that suits you and your book.

3. spark.adobe.com/make/book-cover-maker/

Adobe Spark offers a collection of templates that you can easily adapt to your book cover. There are many creative options to pick from when browsing the Adobe Spark gallery. Moreover, this book cover creator offers an array of customization tools that will allow you to create a design that is unique to your book theme. You can get all of this customization and personalization done with just your mouse and your keyboard.

4. fotor.com

Fotor has a dedicated book cover creator that makes it very easy for you to design attractive and professional-looking book covers from templates. Fotor understands that a good book cover is a great way to boost book sales and they have made it a priority to make it easy for you to achieve.

All you have to do is open Fotor and click on the design feature. Select a book cover size that suits your project and select from an array of templates with dropdowns where you can upload your photos or images and superpose them on the template. Fotor allows you to edit overlays, backgrounds, and stickers. When you are done, you can preview your work and export the project in the file format that works for you.

5. postermywall.com

Designing a book cover can get tricky real fast if you don't have the tools that make it easy for you. There are shapes and sizes to consider and you also have to put the theme of your book into consideration. Fictional books differ from non-fiction and they all differ from academic books. All of these formats have a certain kind of design that is expected so you have to keep this in mind during your design. There are no concrete rules to book cover design but with Postermywall, you can get some guidance on what to do to make this process easy.

6. desygner.com

With Desygner book cover creator, you can create great cover art at zero cost. Desygner has hundreds of book cover templates that you can choose from. They are all customizable and you can personalize them based on your requirements. You don't need any design experience to work with Desygner and you can simply make modifications to the templates instantly. They also have templates that you can use for physical books, Wattpad, and Kindle.

There are so many other tools out there that you can use to create great looking book covers but I have covered 6 of the best in the market. There is hardly any other tool or platform that comes with a feature that these 6 don't already possess. After you have created your book cover design, you may want to convert it into a 3D mockup to use in promotions and ads.

Whenever you browse through Amazon and its array of books on sale, you may have noticed how some book covers stand out while others are just drab and in the background. Do you know why? Because the creators of those designs that stand out have used some basic principles that every professional designer knows. These principles are applied to all professionally designed visuals, including book covers. If you want to learn the graphic design secrets that will convert your audience from a passer-by to a reader, read my book **Book Cover Design Formula: Complete DIY Book Cover Design Guide for Self-published and Indie Authors**.

7 Best Free Tools for Creating Your Book Cover 3D Mockups

Wondering how to **create a book mockup online** to promote your eBook in ads, pop-ups, subscription forms, and landing pages? To gain maximum results when doing your eBook promotion, it is important that your digital product looks tangible and valuable.

The good news is you don't need to hire an expensive designer to create your book mockup. If you already have your book cover image, all you need to do is to convert it into a beautiful visual by using one of these FREE and easy-to-use tools.

Create a book mockup online with one of these FREE tools:

1. A cool and free tool that generates good-quality book cover mockups is **absolutecovers.com**. Simply upload your cover image and get the mockup. Click the right button of your mouse to save it to your computer as a PNG file. It's free. You will get a result like this. Looks rather professional. Doesn't it?

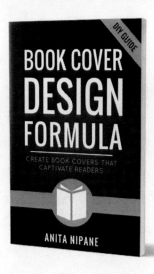

2. A cool tool for generating mockups is also **placeit**. It offers more than 2800 templates to choose from. You can generate a mockup of your book, web page, online course, logo, t-shirt, or even a hat. Actually, there are many more categories. Simply check them out.

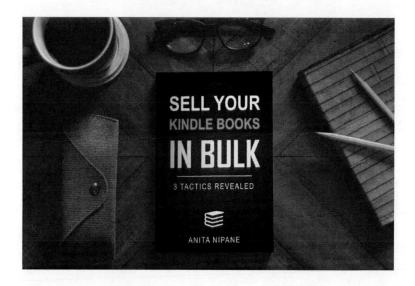

Of course, not all of the templates are for free; however, you can find useful resources also for zero cost. Just sign up and log in. Sure, free services won't give you a large, high-resolution file. However, the quality will be good enough for your website and social media.

3. One more useful tool is **myecovermaker.com**, which will create good quality book and notebook mockups. The advantage of this tool is the option to create book cover mockups for a paperback stack, like in my example, binder, DVD stack, and other interesting formats. You will need to sign in to get access to the free templates.

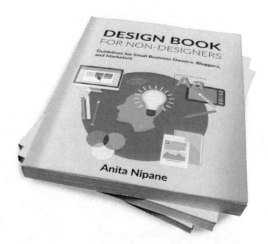

4. If you want to place your book mockup in "a real-life situation" or put your cover on a tablet or a smartphone screen, try the free mockup tool by **adazing.com/cover-mocks**. This is the result you might expect. For an additional

fee, you can get a lifetime access to many other mockups and visuals with your book cover.

5. One of my favorite tools is **magicmockups.com**. You can't create a book cover mockup here, but you can go one step further and visualize how your web page, online course, or even book mockup would look like on a desktop, laptop, or a notepad screen.

6. **bookbrush.com** is a simple and incredibly useful tool for authors. It puts your book cover on the screen of a tablet, smartphone, or on a print book in many creative ways. This tool has a library of premade templates for BookBub ads, Facebook ads, and a lot more. Therefore, you don't have to guess about getting the correct dimensions for your visual. Moreover, if you need to create a mockup for your book series, you will appreciate its Box Set Creator tool that can instantly visualize several books.

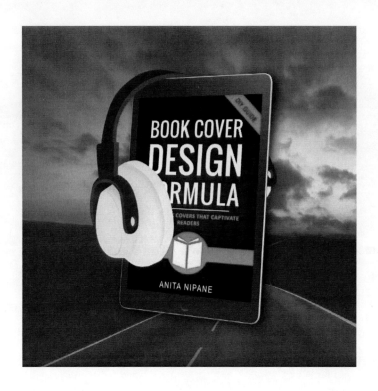

7. Tutorial – Create a Book Cover Mockup with PowerPoint

If you want to be really flexible with creating your book covers and their mockups use PowerPoint. I know, for some of you, it might sound weird... PowerPoint .... and book cover design?!? But it's not weird at all. You will be surprised at what you can actually do with PowerPoint if you know how to... It's just a tool. Similarly, like PhotoShop, Adobe Illustrator, Canva, GIMP, or whatever... You can create a crappy book cover with PhotoShop and an amazing one with PowerPoint. And vice versa. Everything depends on your skills and know-hows... For example, the book cover below and its mockups are created completely in PowerPoint. Who could tell that?

Are you interested? **Go here www.promo.digginet.com** to get access to **9 pre-designed PowerPoint templates** that you can customize for creating mockups and promo visuals for your own books. Additionally, you will get access to a free eBook with **26 Tips for Creating Professionally Looking Book Cover Designs**. Remember that it is important to create a good quality book cover **before** you start working on its mockup. Because having a poor one might significantly reduce your book's success.

10 Free Online Tools That Will Help You Create Your Own Color Schemes

Do you know that almost 93 percent of customers make purchase decisions based on color and visual appearance? Therefore, choosing the right colors for your logo, brand, and product packaging is essential. When you choose colors to represent your business and then use them consistently over time, your brand will become associated with those colors, because color is one of the most-remembered elements of your brand and can make a big impact on how it is perceived. Colors can energize or cool down. They can lead to action and increase your conversation rates online or offline if you learn to use them effectively, or they can scare away your potential customers if used incorrectly. Colors are one of the most powerful design elements. They attract attention, create associations, and set a mood. Actually, you don't need to reinvent the wheel because it is already proven which colors work well together and all professional graphic designers use this knowledge for creating their good-looking designs. You just need to follow the best practices.

There are many free online tools available that can help you choose good-looking color schemes either from your chosen image or following suggestions of these tools. You can even use already finished color schemes that are created by professional designers. Therefore, if you know the basics of color theory, you can always create beautiful designs and color combinations. All you need to do is write down the HEX and RGB codes of the colors you chose to use for your own graphic design projects. Have fun!

1. **sessions.edu/color-calculator** – a free and convenient tool that helps you literally calculate your color schemes. Great tool for creating color schemes using the principles I have described in my book **Graphic Design for Beginners: Fundamental Graphic Design Principles that Underlie Every Design Project**.

2. **coolors.co** – get suggestions for beautiful color schemes with the click of a spacebar.

3. **color.adobe.com** – create color schemes from your image or browse thousands of color combinations. This tool lets you create and save various color schemes, each of which consists of a set of five colors.

4. **http://labs.tineye.com/color** – a great tool for creating a color scheme based on your chosen image. You will get a color palette for all the colors identified in your image, including color codes.

5. Get inspiration from color palettes created by professional designers. Just find the color scheme you like on the website - **colourlovers.com**, copy the codes (hex and RGB) and use them for your designs.

6. **colorzilla.com** - a tool that helps you to get color codes from any point in your Internet browser and use it in your design

projects. Open any web page, analyze it and inspect a palette of its colors.

7. **http://labs.tineye.com/multicolr** – if you need to get free images in a specific color combination, search 20 million Creative Commons images from Flickr by color.

8. **www.color-blindness.com/color-name-hue** – this tool will help you to assign a certain color to the main hue. It comprises 1640 different color names. Try it out.

9. **rgb.to** and **hex.colorrrs.com** – tools for converting color codes from HEX to RGB or CMYK and vice versa.

10 Free Online Logo Maker Tools – Create a Text-Based or Icon Based Logo

If you have a small startup, blog, or other projects that need a logo, you don't need to worry anymore because it's no longer a problem. Nowadays, there are many online logo maker tools that can be used to generate your logo either free of charge or for a small amount of money. Most of them have really advanced logo editing tools that allow you to choose good looking logo icons, adjust colors, sizes, change fonts and download PNG files. Just visit the free online logo maker sites and start creating your logo. However, during the creation process, make sure that your logo reflects your brand's personality and stays simple. Learn more about the principles of good logo design here.

The basic thing you need at least, in the beginning, is your logo in a PNG file with a transparent background, which means you can place it on any other background without having a white square / rectangular background. And you can create one with the help of online logo makers.

Free Logo Online Makers – Make Free Icon-Based Logos Online

Create your icon-based logo online free of charge using the logo maker tools listed below.

1. **freelogodesign.org** – offers different customization variations so that you can design a symbol for your business or blog logo. Add and mix additional shapes, icons, and even logo templates to fully customize your logo. You will get a 200×200 px PNG file for free and eps, pdf, and high-resolution PNG for $39.

2. **logaster.com** - here, you can easily create your logo and get a small size file for free, but if you need a higher resolution file (PNG, pdf, svg, and jpeg), then it's a paid service. Depending on your needs, you will have to pay from $9.99 to $24.99. They also offer brand kits and other products for additional money.

3. **logotypemaker.com** – use their logo templates, edit and customize them and create your free logo; however, attribution is required. You must add a link from their website to yours to use your free logo. If you don't want to make attribution, pay for the premium logo for $24.99.

4. **logogarden.com** – great selection of symbols, fonts, and possibilities to edit and adapt your unique logo. Get a free low-

resolution logo in jpg format. $12.50 for a high-resolution logo, and $39.99 for a vector file.

5. logocraft.com – online logo creator. Choose one of their cliparts and add your text. You can access the logos you create anytime and edit them further.

6. onlinelogomaker.com – simple logo designs. Create your own logo and get a free PNG file.

Free Text-Based Logo Online Makers

If you need a logo that is text-based with no symbols, try using these free tools.

7. supalogo.com – a tool for creating a text-based logo for free. Very simple to use. You can even look at samples, click edit and start from there. When done, download your PNG file.

8. cooltext.com – choose your design and adapt it according to your needs. When finished, download its PNG file for free.

9. flamingtext.com – offers some interesting designs for text-based logos. Free to use however you like. To remove their watermark, you will have to pay starting from $2.99 (for up to five logos a month). Good choice if you need to generate several logos.

10. textcraft.net – generates text-based logos with different textures and colors. You can download it as a PNG file and use however you want.

Let Artificial Intelligence Create Your Logo Design

The pace of progress in artificial intelligence (AI) is incredibly fast. Especially in marketing. You already know that there are tons of online tools that can generate simple logos for your business. But did you know that some of them use artificial intelligence to emulate the work of a professional designer and can create original logos and even simple brand kits? The five AI logo maker tools that I have listed below can be handy if you want to create a new logo or just get some inspiration. Although, they are not free; these tools are interesting enough to be checked out because by using any of them, you can significantly decrease your branding design costs.

1. **logoshi.com** – this is a fun tool that can be used in several creative ways. Insert your business name, slogan, initials and choose colors, and its AI logo designer will generate countless variations of your logo to choose from. Moreover, you can use any of the 1.3 million icons it provides. Select the one you like and edit it until you achieve the result you are looking for. But if you want to create something more original, draw a simple sketch of your logo or even just a few doodles and see what this tool will generate for you. It might be a fun experience.

2. **tailorbrands.com** – this is a similar AI logo design tool that in some cases can substitute a professional designer. Simply

choose your industry, write a few words about your business, select the style of your logo and wait for the virtual AI designer to create it. Moreover, you can use this tool to generate a simple landing page for your business. You will need to pay a monthly subscription though, therefore it could rather be a good solution for a short-term project.

3. **looka.com** - one more AI logo generator that can generate a list of interesting logo designs. You will need to start by choosing the preferred style, icons, and colors for your logo. And the tool will do the rest.

4. **logoai.com** – a simple and very user-friendly tool that uses AI to create logo designs. Just enter your logo name and let their AI logo designer take over from there.

5. **brandbuilder.ai** – if you don't feel that a logo is enough, and you also need a brand book and branding guidelines, try out this tool. You can either create a brand book and social media kit for your already existing logo or create a new logo and brand book from scratch. Having a brand book will make your and your designer's life much easier. Because it will give you a solid framework to use as a starting point for creating your visuals. Therefore, all your communication will be relevant and related to your brand's goals. So, maybe it's worth checking out.

So, as you see, it has never been easy creating a logo and even a brand book. Nowadays the design process is much more accessible to everyone and these tools can be of great help to people who need to get something off the ground quickly.

9 Resources to Find the Perfect Free Stock Video Footage

Did you know that you don't have to record your own videos to create a presentation, slideshow, or social media post? You can use free stock videos, edit and customize them according to your needs with free video editors. Just download the free video you like from one of the websites I have listed below and then edit it, add music, texts and effects with a free video editing tool. Read on to find out more.

Here I have listed 9 resources you can use to get free stock videos. As with free stock images be careful regarding their licenses and before using them check out if the video you have chosen can be used free of charge for personal or commercial purposes.

1. **videvo.com** - an extensive library of over 15,000 free stock footage and motion graphics clips, that is continuously growing. Download their free videos and use them in any project and media.
2. **videos.pexels.com** - completely free videos that are licensed under the Creative Commons Zero (CC0) license. This means you can edit or change the videos and use them free for personal and even for commercial projects.

3. **videezy.com** - download, edit, and remix videos for personal and commercial use, but give credit back to the author.

4. **pixabay.com/videos** - free for commercial use. No attribution required.

5. **vidsplay.com** - can be used for both personal and commercial projects for free; however, a credit link to Vidsplay.com must be added.

6. **mazwai.com** – can be used under attribution license 3.0 (you have to credit the author)

7. **vimeo.com/groups/freehd** - all clips you find in this group can be used for free. In case you have questions, contact their author.

8. **coverr.co** - you can copy, modify, and distribute these videos, even for commercial purposes, all without asking for permission.

9. **YouTube Creative Commons** - use content created by somebody else to make your own videos. All you need do is to go to YouTube search and use their filter to find videos that are given the Creative Commons license. When you find the video, download it to your computer with a tool like **keepv.id** or similar.

winter car drift		🔍

⇄ FILTER

UPLOAD DATE	TYPE	DURATION	FEATURES	SORT BY
Last hour	Video	Short (< 4 minutes)	Live	**Relevance**
Today	Channel	Long (> 20 minutes)	4K	Upload date
This week	Playlist		HD	View count
This month	Film		Subtitles/CC	Rating
This year	Programme		**Creative Commons** ✕	
			360°	
			VR180	
			3D	
			HDR	
			Location	
			Purchased	

When you have chosen your video, customize and edit it in **Youtube Editor** or any other video editor tool. Just upload your video file, add music, publish it on YouTube as a private or public video and share it with your friends or customers.

If you don't want to upload it to YouTube and need some more sophisticated features, use **Windows Movie Maker**, which is designed for Windows Operating Systems (OS). You will be able to crop and edit your video, add texts and effects and use other functionality of the software for free. **iMovie** is alternative software for iOS and macOs. It will help you to create stunning 4K-resolution movies. You can even start editing on iPhone or iPad, then finish on your Mac.

To edit videos on your smartphone **PowerDirector** (Android,

Apple) is a great app. You will be able to crop your videos, change their size and add various artistic effects. Once finished, share them directly to your social media profile or save in your files for use later.

4 YouTube Intro and Outro Videos Makers

Creativity and innovation are at the heart of any successful video. Look at famous YouTubers and you'll notice consistency in their creative works. That's one of the top reasons why they have millions of views and subscribers. The introduction is a make or breakpoint. Have a boring start and the viewer will leave almost immediately; get a captivating introduction and the viewers will be curious about what you'll say next. To help you get the perfect video intro and outro for your YouTube channel or business, there are various video editing tools available. Below are three essential tools that can help you get many views and followers from your videos.

Why an intro video?
- To introduce yourself
- To have a brief description of your brand
- To stimulate interest in the main content

Why an outro video?
- To promote your call to action
- To provide your audience with your social media channels and website address
- To introduce your other videos that might interest them

1. **placeit.com** - those who have used PlaceIt have enjoyed many exciting features. What's in store for you? A wide range of templates, creative customization options, ease of use, and fast and efficient. You don't need hours to create the intro and outro video. Take the shortest time possible so that you can focus on the main content.

2. **canva.com** - a fun webpage to get you started. Never worked on video editing before? The site has simple navigation features that will allow you to create a perfect intro and outro, without having to use complex video creation tools. With thousands of templates available, Canva will enable you to make the most professional looking intro and outro, instantly.

3. **invideo.com** - a great tool for converting your content into perfect videos. Open your web browser and log in to the InVideo page, choose your preferred template or create a personalized one, customize it, and export to your preferred social media site.

4. **introcave.com** - a tool that will show its watermark when you're using the free version. However, if you're willing to go for the paid version, you'll be able to create HD and crystal-clear videos. There are many effects that you can add

to the videos as well to make them aesthetic.

9 Free Online Tools to Create Animated GIFs and Banners

If a picture tells a thousand words, then an animated GIF can tell a whole story. Whether you want to animate your avatar, create an ad banner, or just entertain your friends with a funny photo sequence, an animated GIF is a great way to do it. I have listed 10 free tools you can use to create your own animated GIFs, banners or share already existing GIF animations created by others to express your emotions and attitude.

1. **giphy.com/create/gifmaker** – create animated GIFs from video files and YouTube links, add animated stickers, fun filters, and captions. Moreover, you can combine your pictures and GIFs to create animated GIF slideshows and funny GIF mashups.

2. **ezgif.com/maker** – upload your images or videos, add effects to create your personalized GIFs. Resize, crop, and optimize the file size.

3. **makeagif.com** – keep all your GIFs in one place, create animated GIFs from your pictures, videos, or webcam records.

4. **freegifmaker.me** – have you ever wondered how an animation looks in reverse order? Reverse any GIF file and

get some fun to share with your friends. You can create your own GIFs as well.

5. **picasion.com** – upload your pictures or grab them from **Flickr** or **Picasa Web**, make avatars or funny animations and post them to Tumblr, MySpace, Hi5, Facebook, eBay, Orkut, Bebo, Digg, Friendster, etc.

6. **gickr.com** – just upload your pictures or grab them from your Flickr. Create funny flashy slideshows with you and your friends, cartoons, previews, banners, etc. Post them anywhere you can post pictures: MySpace, Bebo, HI5, etc.

7. **imgflip.com/images-to-gif** – make animated GIFs from video files, YouTube, or images.

8. **webestools.com** – go to Animated Banners Maker, choose your background image either from the banners gallery, the internet, or your computer. Set up a text for each frame of your animated banner (choose the color, font, size, and position of the text) and the frame duration before passing to the next frame. You can make up to 5 frames.

9. **bannernow.com** – choose one of their professionally designed templates and customize it or create your banner from scratch. Add effects, buttons, texts, and design elements and create beautiful and sophisticated designs.

5 Animation Makers for Engaging Social Media Posts

Animated social media content is very effective for engaging the audience. Animations allow you to present your content and concepts in a simple and attractive manner. Back in the day, the high cost was a reason why businesses avoided animated social media contents but thanks to the many new tools that exist today, creating this kind of content is simpler and easier than ever. If you have a digital presence, you need more engagement and traffic, and the following tools will help you achieve that.

1. crello.com

Crello is one of the best online tools that you can use for creating animated content for social media. Use their pre-designed animations, objects, and backgrounds to create eye-catching videos and images for social media, web, blogs, and ads.

2. canva.com

Canva is a very famous online graphics tool thanks to its diverse functionality - which I have mentioned several times in this book. Many of its features you can use for free; but if you get Canva's paid version you get access also to its animator tool that provides different animation effects, like, bounce, slide, fade, 3D, and other effects. Try it for free and decide if it's a good fit for you.

3. pixteller.com

Pixteller is an easy-to-use online image editor and animation maker that can be used to create banners, quote images, photo collages, animated gifs, and more. This tool has a quality designer that will let you create wonderful designs and animated content within seconds. It even has a range of free templates.

4. spark.adobe.com

Adobe Spark is a mobile and web-based application that enables people to make short videos, graphics, and animated content using tools that are very easy to grasp and use. It is a great free service that offers many options for creating perfect animated social media content.

5. animoto.com

Animoto is an online graphic and animation creating tool. Make photos, videos, or animations whenever and however you want using the awesome features that this tool offers. It is quick, effective and even if you don't have a background in graphic design or video making and editing, you can get a professional result.

5 Tools to Take and Annotate Screenshots and Record Screencasts

Sure, you can take screenshots using the screenshot or capturing capability that is already built in your computer, but sometimes more advanced tools can help you do that quicker and easier. These tools can capture only the active browser window, a portion of the screen, or even an entire Web page (beyond just what appears in your browser window). You can crop and annotate the taken screenshots without saving them on your computer and edit them additionally. In simple words, they save your time. Moreover, there are free tools that can help you to record an entire screencast video that you will be able to use, for example, as a tutorial or user guide. I have listed some of them below.

1. **Awesome screenshots** (browser extension for Chrome and Firefox) – capture all or a part of any web page. Add comments, blur sensitive info, and share with one-click uploads. It also includes a built-in editor for adding annotations, shapes, and pointers.

2. **FireShot** (browser extension for Chrome) – take full webpage screenshots. Capture, edit and save them to PDF/JPEG/GIF/PNG, upload, print, send to OneNote, clipboard, or email.

3. **Nimbus Screenshot** (nimbusweb.me/screenshot.php) – another good browser-based option. Available on Chrome, Firefox, and as a Windows desktop application. You can take a screenshot of the entire browser window, a selected region, or an entire webpage, and built-in tools allow you to annotate and edit screenshots. The desktop version adds screen casting functions for recording video clips.

4. **recordit.co** will record everything that happens on your screen as well as your voice. A free and simple solution for recording a tutorial video.

5. **screenpresso.com** – captures your desktop (screenshots and HD videos) for your training documents, collaborative design work, IT bug reports, and anything you need. It is a light-weight screen capturing tool with a built-in image editor, user guide generator, and sharing options.

Add Thousands of Free Fonts to Your Computer

Choosing fonts is an important part of the design process. Fonts can help you emphasize the mood and emotions of the message you want to convey to your audience. The bad news is that the selection of standard fonts that are available on your computer is limited. The good news is that you can add new fonts to your computer easily and free of charge. There is really a wide variety of fonts available in different resources.

10 Free Font Resources to Improve your Designs

1. **fonts.google.com** – search by numerous font categories and choose exactly what you like.
2. **dafont.com** – browse fonts by alphabetical listing, by style, by author, or by popularity.
3. **1001freefonts.com** – Graffiti, Halloween, Gothic, Fantasy – these are just a few of the fancy font categories you can choose from. Check them out!
4. **fontspace.com** – a collection of over 31,000 free fonts shared by designers around the world.
5. **fontsquirrel.com** – hand-selected typefaces that are presented in an easy-to-use format.

6. **urbanfonts.com/free-fonts.htm** – nearly 8,000 free fonts to choose from.

7. **fontzone.net** – thousands of free fonts to enhance your own websites, documents, greeting cards, and more. You can browse popular fonts by themes, name, or style.

8. **fontbundles.net** – beautiful and stylish fonts that you can get for free.

9. **behance.net/collection/4860923/Free-Fonts** – huge selection of stylish fonts. Pay with a Tweet and get any of them.

10. **ffonts.net** – choose from 14 000 fonts and use them as you wish.

Actually, it is very easy to add a new font to your computer. You don't need to be a tech geek or a designer to do that. Just go to any website that I listed before, choose the font you like, and download it. Watch a video tutorial here.

New and amazing fonts are invented every time, and their number keeps growing by the day. There are thousands of different fonts with new ones being constantly created. It's easy to get distracted and select fonts randomly just by making assumptions that "they look good together." But are you sure? There are some basic guidelines that will show you what to look for when trying to find fonts that complement each other. Learn more about the principles of pairing fonts in my book **Graphic Design for Beginners:**

Fundamental Graphic Design Principles that Underlie Every Design Project.

Conclusion

Congratulations! Thank you very much for reading all the way to the end. You've made it through the book and now be able to save your money and time on creating content for web and social media. Hopefully, you got some tips and insights from this book that will stick with you forever. Even if it was only one helpful tip, it might create a big difference in your future design projects.

Thanks for reading! **Please leave a review** so I know what you enjoyed the most about this book and can improve its content - if you felt like something was missing. If you want to be notified when I publish new books, please **follow me on Amazon**.

I don't know if you saw it at the beginning of this book, but I have a **gift** available for you, and I want to remind you that it's still here. You just have to enter your email address to sign up for my online course **19 FREE Tools to Create Visuals for Web and Social Media**. Usually, it costs $30 but you can get it for free.

Since I get asked all the time what tools and resources I use to self-publish my books and create content for social media, I have published a list of my favorite ones on my blog. Check them out here.

Be creative and have fun!

Other Kindle Books by the Author

Free Online Tools Series
- 100+ Free Online Tools to Get Things Done Quicker
- 100+ Free Tools to Create Content for Web & Social Media
- 200 Free Tools to Save Time on Social Media Managing: Boost Your Social Media Results & Reduce Your Hours

Be Your Own Designer Series
- How to Create a Logo? Fundamental Principles of Effective Logo Design
- Graphic Design for Beginners: Fundamental Graphic Design Principles that Underlie Every Design Project

Sell Books on Amazon Series
- 5 Secret Strategies of Kindle Publishing: Earn Passive Income with Non-fiction Books
- Book Cover Design Formula: Create Book Covers That Captivate Readers
- Book Launch Formula: 3 Proven Strategies to Launch Your Non-Fiction Book on Amazon
- Email Marketing for Authors Made Simple: The 1 Page List Building Plan
- Plan Out Your Non-fiction Book Series

UDEMY Online Courses by the Author

- The Ultimate Guide to Creating Your Book Cover Design
- Create Effective Logo for Your Start-up or Blog
- 19 Free Tools to Create Visuals for Web & Social Media

Made in United States
North Haven, CT
07 December 2023

45230074R00045